IN AMERICA EACH MAN HAS A PECULIAR, INALIENABLE RIGHT TO LIVE IN HIS OWN HOUSE IN HIS OWN WAY. HE IS A PIONEER IN EVERY SENSE OF THE WORD. HIS HOME ENVIRONMENT MAY FACE FORWARD, MAY PORTRAY HIS CHARACTER, TASTES, AND IDEAS, IF HE HAS ANY. AND EVERYMAN HERE HAS SOME SOMEWHERE ABOUT HIM.

— FRANK LLOYD WRIGHT

AUSGEFÜHRTE BAUTEN UND ENTWÜRFE VON FRANK LLOYD WRIGHT, 1910

FRANK LLOYD WRIGHT'S
LIFE AND HOMES

⊞ CARLA LIND ⊞

AN ARCHETYPE PRESS BOOK
POMEGRANATE COMMUNICATIONS, INC.

Library of Congress Cataloging-in-Publication Data

Lind, Carla.

Frank Lloyd Wright's life and homes / Carla Lind.

      p.   cm.

"An Archetype Press book."

Includes bibliographical references.

ISBN 978-1-56640-996-4

1. Wright, Frank Lloyd, 1867–1959. 2. Wright, Frank Lloyd, 1867–1959 — Homes and haunts — United States. 3. Architects — United States — Biography. I. Title.

NA737.W7L52 1994   94-7923

720'.92–dc20   CIP

Published by

Pomegranate Communications, Inc.

Box 808022, Petaluma, CA

94975-8022

Catalogue no. A727

Produced by Archetype Press, Inc.

Project Director: Diane Maddex

Designer: Robert L. Wiser

5 6 7 8 9 10 11 12

Printed in Singapore

Opening photographs: Page 1: Frank Lloyd Wright at Taliesin about 1937. Page 2: Wright's office in his Oak Park studio. Pages 6–7: Taliesin West at the foot of the McDowell Mountains.

CONTENTS

Wright at Taliesin about 1924.
Finding inspiration all around,
he studied the writings of
Emerson and Whitman, the
theories of the Arts and
Crafts movement, the simplicity of the Japanese, and the
ruins of ancient civilizations.

E WAS AMERICA'S MOST CELEBRATED
architect, but like his father, uncle, and grandfathers before him, Frank Lloyd Wright was also a preacher. He
preached through his buildings, his writings, and his lectures. His gospel was unity, democracy, simplicity, in-
tegrity, and individuality. He wanted to save the world
from mediocre, inappropriate buildings. Architecture was
not just his job; it was his life's obsession.

He was also a revolutionary. As a young man,
Wright decided that what America needed was an au-
thentic architecture—one based on the values, lifestyles,
landscapes, and ingenuity found in the United States. A
conscientious student of life, Wright had an uncanny abil-
ity to absorb and combine experiences and inspirations
and find their common truths. They became ingredients
in his own creative caldron from which he would pour
forth his recipe for architecture.

By 1900 Wright had formulated his own philoso-
phy of organic architecture, which over the next half cen-
tury was expressed in a multitude of designs but never
changed in substance. His early houses were called Prairie

America, more than any other nation, presents a new architectural proposition, her ideal is democracy. And in democratic spirit her institutions are professedly conceived. This means that she places a premium upon individuality—the highest possible development of the individual consistent with a harmonious whole.... Frank Lloyd Wright

Ausgeführte Bauten und Entwürfe von Frank Lloyd Wright, 1910

Style, some built in the 1920s were known as textile block, and those designed in the last two decades he named Usonian—but the principles remained the same.

Wright had a prolific career, designing for more than seven decades and completing nearly five hundred structures, eighty percent of which were residential. Considering that each building usually included numerous custom-designed decorative arts—from art glass to furniture—his output was amazing and his versatility unmatched. He designed skyscrapers and weed holders, entire cities and magazine covers, textiles and windmills.

As he built, Wright preached. He wrote and lectured about his design theories with equal enthusiasm and was particularly effective in inspiring young people. His words as much as his buildings taught America about appropriate architecture. He offered open floor plans rather than boxes within boxes. He sited a building carefully to maximize the pleasures of interaction between the inside and outside. He sought ways to put good architecture within the reach of the average citizen. He respected the essence of each building material and used technology to cut costs and improve living spaces. He called this organic architecture because it grew from the nature of the site, the nature of the materials, and the nature of the clients and their needs.

Wright's personal life was often dramatic and publicly scrutinized. Born in 1867, he died before his ninety-second birthday in 1959. Married three times, he had seven natural children and one stepchild. His financial affairs were usually a disaster, but thanks to understanding patrons and frustrated creditors he always lived well. Somehow he bought grand pianos, handmade saddles, well-tailored clothes, custom automobiles, and Japanese art whether he had the money or not.

Beginning in 1898, when he added his studio to his Oak Park house, his home life and work life were integrated. For the last three decades of his life, he enjoyed the benefits of a communal lifestyle in which he was surrounded by devoted apprentices who were his associates, his students, and his laborers. His three residences became lively, evolving laboratories for his radical design concepts and are now National Historic Landmarks.

▓ Frank Lloyd Wright, you are part and parcel of the wonder-making pioneer spirit of our people. . . . Your works, your thoughts ever soar above pedestrian paths. A blithe spirit, 'with more Puck than of Ariel,' you design your buildings as if they were to take their place in a happier world—one of light, of grace, of gaiety—and for human beings . . . who live in a world where . . . the pioneer concept of democracy seems a reality. ▓

Ralph Walker
Gold Medal Presentation,
National Institute of Arts
and Letters, 1953

A NATURAL CHILDHOOD

FROM HIS EARLY YEARS FRANK LLOYD Wright's mother encouraged him to become a builder of great buildings. Foremost were lessons about the natural world and the order and harmony found there. Spending summers on his uncles' farms in the rolling hills of the Wisconsin River valley, Wright learned about hard work as well as the rhythms of nature. These experiences were the most important influence in his life. Unity and truth— the ideals to which the Lloyd Jones family was devoted— became integral to the young Wright's training.

When Wright was nine, his mother introduced him to the Froebel gifts. Created by the inventor of Kindergarten, they taught the laws of nature through geometry. Wright often acknowledged the impact these blocks had on his architecture. His father taught him to share his love of music, an art form parallel to architecture. The son eventually composed his buildings as one would compose a symphony.

Wright briefly studied engineering at the University of Wisconsin and worked part-time as a draftsman. Soon, it became apparent that he had to get a better-paying job.

Wright's maternal Lloyd Jones clan gathered in 1883. Frank is to the right of the empty chair, holding his sister Maginel. His sister Jane is behind to the left, in front of his mother, Anna, and father, William Russell Carey Wright. The family included farmers, teachers, and ministers—all devoted Unitarians. Wright's father was an avid musician as well as a minister. He and Anna later divorced.

THE OAK PARK YEARS

Wright and his family posed in 1890 on the front steps of his new Oak Park home. Catherine Wright, holding baby Lloyd, is at center. Between her and Frank are his mother, Anna, and sister Maginel. Five more children would be added in the next thirteen years. Many of Wright's early commissions resulted from contacts made in his Oak Park neighborhood or at the church of his Uncle Jenkin Lloyd Jones (far left).

UPON HIS ARRIVAL IN CHICAGO IN 1887, Wright was hired by Joseph Lyman Silsbee, an architect whose clients included one of Wright's uncles. Within a year Wright had a new job with the prestigious firm of Adler and Sullivan. Wright called Louis Sullivan his *lieber Meister,* acknowledging that he was his greatest teacher. Sullivan's artistry was especially apparent in his use of integral — as opposed to applied — ornament inspired by nature.

Wright soon met a beautiful, red-haired, sixteen-year-old-girl, Catherine Tobin, at his uncle's church and married her in 1889. He designed a home for them in Oak Park, a Chicago suburb, and continually remodeled it as the family grew. After a disagreement with Sullivan, Wright established his own practice. From 1893 to 1909 he received two hundred fifty commissions, resulting in 142 buildings — a remarkable achievement.

By 1909 Wright was growing restless. He responded to a German publisher's request to work on a publication of his work. Closing his practice, he and Mamah Borthwick Cheney, a former client, left their families and sailed for Europe to begin a new life together.

TURBULENT TIMES

WRIGHT RETURNED TO THE UNITED States in 1910, after one year abroad, and reestablished a practice in Chicago. He also began construction on a retreat in his beloved Wisconsin hills near Spring Green, a home he called Taliesin. There he and Mamah Borthwick Cheney lived until a crazed servant murdered her, her two children, and four employees and set the house on fire.

Within months, the traumatized Wright met Miriam Noel, who eventually became his second wife. She accompanied him to Tokyo when he worked on the Imperial Hotel from 1916 to 1922. But with a chaotic personal life and uncertain economic times, Wright's career remained adrift. When he met a beautiful Montenegran dancer, Olgivanna Hinzenberg, he found the spiritual sustenance he was seeking. She was thirty years younger with an eight-year-old daughter, Svetlana, who would soon be joined by their child, Iovanna.

This first Taliesin was partly destroyed by fire in 1914 and then again in 1925. Despite financial and legal struggles that enveloped Wright, Taliesin—and Wright—emerged from the ashes.

REVITALIZATION

Surrounded by students at the Taliesin Fellowship, Wright could teach every day. Picnic lunches for apprentices and guests such as this one in 1940 were highlights of many summer days in Wisconsin. During the Depression there was little work, but Wright wrote and focused on his vision of a decentralized society that he called Broadacre City. As part of this concept, he developed the Usonian house.

AT AN AGE WHEN MOST MEN WOULD be considering retirement, Wright began a second career, calling on the preacher and teacher within him. First, he delivered two lecture series, one at Princeton and the other at the Art Institute of Chicago. They presented his mature, visionary ideas of what architecture should be. Soon after, *An Autobiography* was published. This introduced more people to his individualism and let the world know he was still around.

In 1932 the Wrights established the Taliesin Fellowship, an architectural school where the students shared housekeeping and farming as well as design and construction tasks. An idea for a permanent winter residence grew out of an earlier temporary camp they had constructed in the Arizona desert. Taliesin West, begun near Scottsdale in 1937, became their winter home.

If there were any doubts about Wright's regenerative powers, two highly acclaimed commissions—the Johnson Wax Administration Building and Fallingwater—reestablished him in the 1930s as a great architect, eager to compete with the new International Style.

FINAL CHALLENGES

ONCE WORLD WAR II WAS OVER, WRIGHT was able to put his community planning ideas to work at cooperative enclaves in Detroit, Galesburg and Kalamazoo, Michigan, and Pleasantville, New York. While most of his designs continued to be residences, large and small, he was awarded several noteworthy public commissions. For nearly sixteen years Wright worked on the Guggenheim Museum in New York, for a while living in a suite at the Plaza Hotel, which he called Taliesin East. He was also retained to design the campus of Florida Southern University, the Price Tower in Bartlesville, Oklahoma, the Marin County Civic Center in California, and several churches.

At the time of his death in 1959, Frank Lloyd Wright had been awarded nearly a thousand commissions and was a highly honored and acclaimed man. His work had been exhibited around the world, and he had published numerous articles and books. But most important, he had successfully altered our collective thinking about what a home could be and challenged us to cherish our individuality and find wisdom in nature.

Wright frequently visited his homes at Usonia in Pleasantville, New York. Here he inspects a foundation with architect Aaron Resnick. Like many of his 1950s designs, these houses were more fluid and not as rectilinear as Wright's earlier work, using circles and curves more freely. During this period the Taliesin Fellowship flourished. Together Wright and his apprentices worked on scores of projects, nearly a hundred while Wright was in his nineties.

1856 Lloyd Jones family settles in the Wisconsin River valley and eventually acquires 1,800 acres

1867 Frank Lloyd Wright is born June 8 in Richland Center, Wisconsin, to Anna and William Russell Carey Wright, a minister

1876 Anna Wright purchases the Froebel gifts for Frank

1879 After moving from church to church, the Wrights come to Madison, where William opens a music conservatory. Frank spends summers on his uncles' farms

1884 William and Anna divorce. Frank never sees his father again

1886 Wright attends the University of Wisconsin

1887 Wright comes to Chicago and is employed by Joseph Lyman Silsbee

1888–92 Adler and Sullivan employ Wright until he is discovered designing "bootleg" houses after hours

1889 Wright marries Catherine Lee Tobin. They build a home in Oak Park, a Chicago suburb

1890 The first of their six children, Frank Lloyd Wright, Jr., is born

1893 Wright opens his own practice in Steinway Hall

1898 A studio is added to the Oak Park home, uniting Wright's personal and professional lives. His practice thrives

1900 Wright designs his first Prairie Style house

1905 Frank and Catherine Wright make their first trip to Japan

1907 Wright has his first solo exhibit at the Art Institute

1908 "In the Cause of Architecture," a statement of Wright's theories, is published in *Architectural Record*

1909 Wright sails for Europe with Mamah Borthwick Cheney, leaving his wife of twenty years and six children. He works on the *Ausgeführte Bauten und Entwürfe,* published by Wasmuth in 1910

1911 The first Taliesin, Wright's retreat near Spring Green, Wisconsin, is begun

Known for his unconventional dress and self-confident presence, Wright was frequently photographed. These portraits show him at ages three, twenty, forty-nine, and seventy-one.

Wright, aged eighty-six, guides the installation of his retrospective exhibition in 1953 on the site of the Guggenheim Museum.

1914 Tragedy hits Taliesin when Mamah Borthwick Cheney, her children, and four others are killed and the house is set on fire

1915 Miriam Noel, who will become Wright's second wife, moves to Taliesin

1916–22 Wright spends most of his time in Tokyo working on the Imperial Hotel

1923 Anna Lloyd Wright dies. Catherine Wright divorces Frank, fourteen years after their separation, and he marries Miriam Noel

1923–25 Wright briefly establishes an office in California, completing five commissions supervised by his son Lloyd, four of them using the textile-block method

1925 Wright meets Olga Ivanovna (Olgivanna) Lazovich Hinzenberg. Their daughter, Iovanna, is born. Another fire strikes Taliesin

1927 Wright divorces Miriam Noel after a three-year separation. He becomes incorporated to settle his financial problems and begins his autobiography

1928 Wright marries Olgivanna when his divorce is final

1930 The Kahn lectures at Princeton sum up forty years of Wright's architectural theories

1932 Wright's first autobiography is published (revised in 1943). He and Olgivanna establish the Taliesin Fellowship

1935–36 The Fallingwater and Johnson Wax commissions breathe new life into his career. The first

Usonian house is designed, and the Broadacre City model is built

1937 Work begins on Taliesin West

1949 Wright receives the AIA Gold Medal, one of numerous awards and honorary degrees

1950s Wright designs many houses and public buildings, notably the Guggenheim Museum in New York

1951 The Sixty Years of Living Architecture exhibition opens in Philadelphia and then tours the world, returning to New York in 1953

1958 Wright publishes *The Living City*, his last book, about the Broadacre City concept

1959 Wright dies two months before his ninety-second birthday

1985 Olgivanna Wright dies

HOME AND STUDIO

OAK PARK, ILLINOIS. 1889 - 1909

Wright's innovative design for his Oak Park studio served as a public advertisement. His artful use of geometric forms is seen in the three-dimensional entrance composition as well as in delicate art glass created for the playroom.

IN 1889 TWENTY-TWO-YEAR-OLD FRANK Lloyd Wright and his new bride, Catherine Tobin, eighteen years old, purchased a corner lot in Oak Park, a growing area just west of Chicago. Influenced by the picturesque Shingle Style popularized by his former employer Joseph Lyman Silsbee, Wright built an efficient six-room home with a steeply pitched roof, curved verandas, and projecting bays all wrapped with wood shingles and grounded by masonry garden walls.

The plan of the house was somewhat traditional, with the living room, dining room, and kitchen radiating from the central fireplace on the first floor. But Wright opened the spaces, beginning his movement to break out of the boxlike rooms that were customary at the time. Walls seemed more like movable Japanese screens. By overlapping rooms, making openings between rooms larger, and wrapping wood bands around the walls, he created a flowing, spacious feeling that reflected his family's informal, casual lifestyle. Within this openness were contrasting intimate spaces such as the inglenook by the fireplace and generous window seats. The color scheme,

Windows in the house were grouped, making them light screens and opening the inside spaces to the outside terraces and garden.

drawn from nature, blends soft greens and golds with the amber tones of the oak trim.

Upstairs, Wright provided a light-filled studio on the front of the house with a master bedroom and nursery to the rear. The bathroom, stairway, and closets were placed to create sound buffers between the primary rooms. Within six years, the Wrights had four children and had stretched the capacity of their cottage.

A major renovation in 1895 included a large two-story addition. The studio became a divided dormitory for the children, and a barrel-vaulted playroom was added so that Catherine could have a nursery school in the home. Its balcony was perfect for dramatic and musical performances, and a grand piano was cleverly tucked under the stairs so that only the keyboard occupied space in the room. Wright was able to extend the space visually beyond the limits of the walls by using skylights, window walls, and a mural over the fireplace. Composed of pure geometric shapes like the Froebel block constructions of his childhood, the playroom was a successful experiment in Wright's home laboratory.

By 1898 Wright decided to add a larger studio to the house to accommodate his growing practice. A potential client would certainly be intrigued by the sculptures of crouched human figures over the entrance, the colonnade of stork panels that led the way into the maze-like entrance, and the embracing loggia lighted from above by three long, intricate art glass panels. Two octagonal rooms—a dramatic two-story drafting room and an intimate library—branched out from the rectangular core that included his office. Specially designed, rectilinear furniture rested on the leatherlike magnesite floor. The excitement of an architectural revolution was everywhere.

After Wright moved out in 1909, many alterations were made. The building was split first into two units for rental income for his family and later into five apartments. Since 1974 the home and studio has undergone complete restoration. It once again appears as it did when Wright lived there and used it as his laboratory, the birthplace of the Prairie School of architecture. It is operated by the Frank Lloyd Wright Home and Studio Foundation and is open to the public.

Wright's design ideas evolved within his own home and studio. The living room (page 30) still retained some classical details, but the dining room (page 31) was his first to integrate furnishings and architecture. Over the fireplace in the playroom (pages 32–33), he collaborated with Orlando Gianinni to create a mural, *The Geni and the Fisherman,* integrating the arts. The controlled octagonal library (opposite), with only clerestory windows, served as an ideal presentation room where Wright would sell his innovative ideas to adventurous clients.

TALIESIN

Winter at Taliesin blankets the milkhouse at Midway farm (above), Frank and Olgivanna Wright (opposite) in 1940, and the living quarters (pages 38–39).

SOON AFTER RETURNING FROM EUROPE, Wright felt the need for a more secluded residence that would allow him privacy. His mother offered him a parcel of land in the Lloyd Jones settlement in Spring Green, Wisconsin. In 1911 he built his new home, Taliesin ("shining brow"), on the side of a hill overlooking the Wisconsin River valley. For the next forty-eight years, Wright lived here, building and rebuilding the horizontal limestone and stucco complex. It was more than a shelter—it was a farm, a school, an architecture studio, and an entertainment center.

In keeping with Wright's concept of organic architecture, Taliesin grew in response to the needs of those who lived here. Three times it was seriously damaged by fire. Currently, the house alone includes nearly 37,000 square feet of space beneath low, red, sheltering roofs, all enhanced by gardens, terraces, and courtyards. Its size belies its simplicity. Carefully sited around the rolling 600-acre property are the Hillside Home School buildings, Tan-y-deri (his sister Jane's house), the Midway farm buildings, assorted smaller residences, and the Romeo and Juliet windmill.

The house is really a series of pavilions connected by passageways, covered and uncovered, with limestone floors continuing throughout. Because the same materials are used inside and out, the transitions are smooth. Low compressed spaces are followed by open releases into dramatic two-story rooms such as the masterful living room. Throughout, the essence of each building material is emphasized, such as stone laid with projecting layers as it is found in the quarry. Light, both natural and artificial, is used to enhance the experience by highlighting and shadowing areas. Windows are either casements, opening out, or fixed glass, often with an invisible mitered joint that dissolves the corner and makes the roof seem to float above. Every room opens to an outdoor space, the most dramatic being the forty-foot-long "bird walk" cantilevered into the treetops from the living room.

Although Wright maintained a small studio in the house, the larger drafting room is in the renovated Hillside Home School, once a boarding school run by his aunts Jane and Ellen. Also housed in the school are the theater, galleries, a dining room, a kitchen, student rooms, and a

Taliesin fits as naturally into the terrain as the materials from which it is built. Natural forms intertwine with built shapes. Long bands of windows frame the views beyond, while cantilevered balconies reach into the trees.

Within the spacious Taliesin are open entertainment areas as well as private retreats such as Wright's studio (page 42) and a corner of the living room (page 43). Despite the energy in the living room (opposite), created from a dynamic interplay of geometric forms, varied textures, and rich colors, the space is harmonious.

living room with one of the most magnificent stone fireplaces in the complex. Rising from the hill behind the school is one of Wright's earliest commissions: a windmill named Romeo and Juliet because of its two embracing forms. Built in 1897 for his aunts—despite the cautions of neighboring farmers more accustomed to windmills with metal frames—it was only recently restored after nearly a hundred years of use.

The Midway farm buildings, located midway between the school and the house, were added in the 1930s and 1940s after the Taliesin Fellowship was formed. Earlier farm buildings were near the home.

The Wrights always enjoyed the company of their family, students, friends, and guests. Clients often were invited to visit Taliesin and participate in the gala Saturday night formals and attend the frequent musical performances. Wright's home life and professional life were one, creating a lively, stimulating atmosphere.

Taliesin, currently operated by the Frank Lloyd Wright Foundation, is open for tours. An extensive restoration of this National Historic Landmark has begun.

TALIESIN WEST

The design of Taliesin West grew from the materials and forms of the desert. Ancient petroglyphs and native vegetation became important elements in shaping the look of the complex.

FIVE YEARS AFTER THE TALIESIN Fellowship was established, the Wrights and their apprentices sought a more hospitable and healthier winter climate. The harsh Wisconsin conditions and the promise of an exciting new building project drew the group to a stretch of undeveloped Sonora desert at the foot of the McDowell Mountains near Phoenix. They named their winter retreat Taliesin West. Inspired by an earlier desert encampment called Ocatilla, the 1937 project had canvas roofs with no glass windows, permitting an intimate relationship with the desert and a constant awareness of the quality of the desert light.

Wright wanted a construction method that would be inexpensive and durable, using indigenous materials. To build the walls, he developed a technique that made use of the colorful boulders scattered around the desert floor. Placed in wooden forms with their flat sides out, the rocks were surrounded by a sandy concrete, and then the forms were removed.

The textures and colors of these ruinlike rubble walls harmonize with the landscape. Huge redwood trusses

At Taliesin West built forms
mirror natural ones. Mountains stand behind canted
rubble walls (pages 48–49);
the bell tower (above) juts
over the horizontal expanse of
the terraces (opposite).

rise from the walls and support the translucent roofs of
the main rooms. The staccato rhythm of this roof struc-
ture is repeated in the dentil edging of the roofs and
tiers of shallow stairs that flow from the buildings. The
dominant shape of the horizontal complex is the trian-
gle—the angle of the roof and walls echoing the slope
of the surrounding mountains. Few, if any, rectangles are
found here.

Skillful contrasts strengthen the design. The hori-
zontality of the rambling complex is accentuated by the
intermittent upward thrusts; the light, open roofs float
above the heavy walls; the subtle sand colors are enhanced by bright red accents; geometric shapes are soft-
ened by natural vegetation; the rough texture of the walls
meets the smoothness of water and glass. It is both a
cloistered retreat and an open, informal camp.

Like its sister Taliesin, Taliesin West was a con-
stantly evolving symphony. Wright was never static, always experimenting, eventually adding glass, replacing the
canvas with translucent, synthetic materials, and using
steel in place of some of the wood supports. The original

plan called for an office, a large drafting room, a garden (living) room, a vault, a kitchen, a dining room, apprentice living quarters, and the Wrights' living quarters. Eventually, a large theater was built to provide better concert space for the frequent musical events. Other spaces have been enclosed, expanded, or added in response to the needs of the Fellowship, which had sixty-five students and family members at its peak in 1946.

Linking all the various architectural elements are outdoor terraces, loggias, courtyards, pools, and fountains—providing sensual variety at every turn. Levels change, shadows are encouraged by the building details, and the natural flora of the area are incorporated into the design of the complex.

Taliesin West was built when Wright was seventy years old and was his part-time residence for the next twenty-two years. It stands as a testament to his lifelong vitality, creativity, and versatility. Today it is still an active place used year-round. The Frank Lloyd Wright Foundation continues to operate a school, an archive, an architectural practice, and a tour program at the site.

The apprentices often put down their T-squares and became construction workers. The living room (page 52) and drafting room (page 53) originally had canvas roofs that gave the complex the look of a ship beached on the sand. Taliesin West was Wright's winter home until his death in 1959, soon after this photograph (opposite) was taken.

⌗ It is the duty of every man to raise the character and tone of his own home . . . to the highest point his capabilities permit. ⌗

Frank Lloyd Wright
The Art and Craft of the Machine, 1894

FURTHER READING

Brooks, H. Allen, ed. *Writings on Wright: Selected Comment on Frank Lloyd Wright.* Cambridge: MIT Press, 1981.

Gill, Brendan. *Many Masks: A Life of Frank Lloyd Wright.* New York: G. P. Putnam's Sons, 1987.

Lind, Carla. *The Wright Style.* New York: Simon and Schuster, 1992.

Meehan, Patrick J., ed. *Frank Lloyd Wright Remembered.* Washington, D.C.: Preservation Press, 1991.

―――. *Truth Against the World: Frank Lloyd Wright Speaks for an Organic Architecture.* Washington, D.C.: Preservation Press, 1992.

Pfeiffer, Bruce Brooks, ed. *Frank Lloyd Wright: The Masterworks.* New York: Rizzoli, 1993.

Secrest, Meryle. *Frank Lloyd Wright: A Biography.* New York: Alfred A. Knopf, 1992.

Twombly, Robert. *Frank Lloyd Wright: An Interpretive Biography.* New York: Harper and Row, 1973.

Wright, Frank Lloyd. Bruce Brooks Pfeiffer, ed. *Collected Writings.* 3 vols. New York: Rizzoli, 1992–94.

Wright, John Lloyd. *My Father, Frank Lloyd Wright.* 1946. New York: Dover Publications, 1992.

ACKNOWLEDGMENTS

The author wishes to thank the Frank Lloyd Wright Home and Studio Foundation Research Center and the Oak Park Public Library.

Archetype Press is grateful to Judith Bromley for assistance with the cover illustration by Robert L. Wiser.

Illustration Sources:

Gordon Beall: 2, 26, 27, 28–29, 30

Richard Bowditch: 40, 41, 42, 46, 47, 48–49, 50

Chicago Historical Society: 1 (Hedrich-Blessing photo HB-04414 1)

Frank Lloyd Wright Home and Studio Foundation: 13 (H&S 203), 14 (H&S H92), 23 top left (H&S 1089), 23 top right (H&S 167)

Pedro E. Guerrero: 19, 20, 24, 37, 44, 54

Hedrich-Blessing, Jon Miller: 31, 32–33, 34

Balthazar Korab Ltd.: 6–7, 51, 52, 53

Library of Congress: 23 bottom right

State Historical Society of Wisconsin: 8, 16–17, 23 bottom left

Elizabeth Zeschin: 43

Scot Zimmerman: 36, 38–39